2016

Other books by the author

Spirit Within and Other Poems

2016

Political Poems

Doris Ervin

All worldwide rights reserved. No part of this work may be reproduced without written permission of the author.

2016 Political Poems

ISBN-978-0-692-83203-5

This book is copyright material and cannot be copied, reproduced, transferred, distributed, leased, licensed or publicly performed or used in any way except as specifically permitted in writing by the author, as allowed under the terms and conditions under which it was agreed or as strictly permitted by applicable copyright law. Any unauthorized distribution or use of this text may be a direct infringement of the author's rights and those responsible may be liable in law accordingly.

Published by Doris Ervin
Denver, Colorado
USA

© 2017 by Doris Ervin

For Barbara Duckworth, a shining example of citizen volunteers, who make this American Democracy work.

CONTENTS

Acknowledgements	xi
A Perfect Storm	1
The Primal Scream	2
9/11 to 2016	4
Blankets for Wall Street	6
Attack from Within	8
Where's the Middle Class	10
Slap Down	13
The Clown and the Jezebel	14
Money Ball	16
From Smoke-Filled Rooms to Twitter	18
Just Lie	19
Fly Overs	20
The Russians are Coming!	23
Punditry, Press, Fake News	24
The Sacred Trust	26
Drain the Swamp	27

CONTENTS

The Political Paradigm	28
A New Normal	31
From Bubbles to Walls	32
Bubbles	33
Gridlock	34
When did We Become Radicalized	35
It is up to Us	36
The Greater Bargain	37
It's More Than Politics	38
Her Story	40
Hillary's Baggage	42
A Meeting in the Woods	44
April 4th, 1968	46
How Many Votes	48

Acknowledgements

Our American Democracy functions best when the greatest number of citizens participate. This book is dedicated to one such citizen volunteer in the election of 2016, Barbara Duckworth, who knocked on over 1000 doors, made 100's of telephone calls, and shepherded her delegate vote from the caucus to numerous Colorado conventions.

I wish to say 'Thank You' to Barbara and to all of the volunteers like her who contribute of themselves to maintain the freedoms all of us enjoy. They inspire the rest of us into action.

The inspiration for this book began when I saw the well-circulated picture of a mother with her daughter on her back, meeting Hillary during a walk in the woods after the election. My poem, 'A Meeting in the Woods,' was the first of this collection. From there, I wanted to investigate in words what led up to and resulted in this historic election. These poems express one citizen's thoughts and reactions to the election of 2016.

Doris Ervin
Denver, Colorado
January, 2017

2016

"Prosperity is necessarily the first theme of a political campaign."

Woodrow Wilson

A Perfect Storm

Technology

The rapidity of technological change in the last forty years may be more than the human psyche can assimilate in one lifetime! It is the good, bad, and ugly in one tiny package. The smartphone: a symbol of the transition of cultures. Were we ready?

Globalization

American businesses went off-shore to exploit less developed countries, not to join hands and celebrate in the oneness of the human race. Now those countries have new, dynamic economies, new infrastructure, factories and increased employment. It was all misplaced for greed, short-term profit for a few. Now there's a big scramble to get it back.

Immigration

Wink, wink is not an immigration policy. It is a loop-hole meant to be exploited by all factions. Other countries protect their borders, their jobs, and their ability to properly assimilate newcomers, with fair, equal and enforceable immigration practices. Why do you suppose the United States cannot?

The Primal Scream

How did we not hear it?
Are we collectively deaf?
Or do we just not care to
hear unless we are directly
effected; selective hearing.

Did we not hear the screams
when there was massive job
losses following the 2008
economic downturn?

Did we not hear the screams
when millions of people lost
their homes perpetuated by
corrupt mortgage companies
and banks?

Did we not hear the screams
when employees were required
to train their replacements for
the foreign migration of jobs?

Did we not hear the screams
of our military men and women
who came home to no jobs, and
in some cases, to less than even
adequate medical treatment?

How did we, all of us,
not hear the screams of
so many displaced people
in our country? Did politicians
become even more tone-deaf
to those they were elected
to serve?

The people, who were so
Adversely affected, heard each
other's screams. The wave grew
and became a critical mass.

They would be heard
in the election of 2016.

9/11 to 2016

Fifteen years of war.
Yes, it is happening 'over there'
in the Middle East, but what is
happening 'over here?'

We 'shocked and awed' them.
We removed a foreign leader.
We 'buddied up' with the Middle
East oil cartel. The negotiated
exchange rate: our soul for oil.

But we're fighting them 'over there.'

American men and women are
killed and maimed. Our national
bank account is drained into debt.
Positive constructive, creative
energy is sucked out of us.

But we're fighting them 'over there.'

War, by nature, is all-consuming
because it assumes a misplaced,
self-proclaimed, solemn, mortal duty:
it kills. It cannot co-exist along-side
anything else of importance. It
dominates, displaces, and demands
the full attention and resources
of a nation.

But we're fighting them 'over there.'

Something slipped away from us
while our heads were turned toward
the Middle East; we lost our innocence.
We are fearful now of many things:
each other, people in different clothes,
getting a job, keeping a job, and
having enough. Our concentration
is temporal.

But we're fighting them 'over there.'

For fifteen years, Americans have lived
with the consequences and results of
war. Many citizens struggle and suffer
with no relief. As the struggle intensifies,
so does the anger.

Yes, we're fighting the war 'over there'
but we're losing the heart of our
nation 'over here.'

Americans are "Mad as Hell."
They cast votes on 11/08/2016.

Blankets for Wall Street

It was late September, 2008.
Banks demanded a government bailout.
When they didn't get it, the stock market
tumbled into record lows and kept tumbling.

Banks, mortgage companies and car
manufacturers demanded a bailout
from the disastrous, direct results of
their own colossal mismanagement.
Their argument was tainted with
blackmail innuendo: *we are too big to fail.*
If we fail, everyone will go down with us.
They got it all: bailouts, TARP, and loans.

Blankets for Wall Street.

Fall turned into Winter. Cold winds blew.
Jobs hemorrhaged, under-water homes
foreclosed, lifetime accumulated
retirement funds disappeared.

The answer: recovery must start from
the top and trickle down to the
struggling masses.

Translation: we take care of ourselves
first and we live lavishly.

Stop! Just Stop!

Before the crash, huge pots of money were
stolen by Wall Street through the use of
derivatives and re-constituted mortgages.

After the crash, bailout and TARP money was stolen by Wall Street. There was no accountability, it was the Wild West, one stagecoach robbery after the other.

Still more blankets for Wall Street.

Hard working, tax-paying American citizens were left out in the cold: no jobs, houses in foreclosure, no retirement funds. Shovel-ready jobs were a sham, another pot of money for Wall Street to steal and steal they did. They shoveled huge amounts of money into their own deep pockets.

Sorry, no more blankets.

American men and women suffered greatly for years in a frigid economic climate: many still suffering. Blocks of unoccupied houses confirmed the hardship and decline. They scurried to find any kind of job to pay any amount of money. There were no bailouts, not for the masses. They were on their own. Their anger smoldered and simmered for eight long years.

In 2016, it boiled over.

Attack from Within

Remember a time when Americans
were wide-eyed, somewhat naive
and innocent; like a loveable puppy,
bouncy, joyful, with no real worries.

Everyone seemed to 'have enough,' to
be comfortable if they worked hard,
and work they did. Loyalty was returned
with lifetime jobs and benefits.

But then, the winds of change began
to blow: downsizing, outsourcing,
off-shore migrations, robots, computers,
temporary workers, contract workers,
piece workers. People began to struggle
to 'have enough.'

September 11, 2001, the United States
was brutally attacked by people who
wanted to kill us, all of us. A dagger
directly into the heart of Americans.

September 2008: The United States
was attacked brutally from within by
mortgage companies, banks and
Wall Street. They didn't care if they
hurt us or not; whether we lived or died.

Many Americans were laid out flat. Some, who lost everything, could not get up. There was no outstretched hand to help them. A few finally struggled to their feet but they stood at barely half their former stature, if that.

They had been badly shaken and with good reason. Politicians, CEOs, board members and shareholders decided to help themselves first without reservation or conscience.

Americans were attacked by Americans.

By 2016, hard-working Americans were ready to explode.

Where's the Middle Class?

Where's the middle class? Gone
the way of drive-in movies,
I suppose.

The gears of the Industrial
Revolution ground to a halt, rusted
in place, and were swept away,
replaced by tiny, shiny chips. The
Technological Age is well underway.
No need now for heft and brawn.
There is new terminology too.

"Exercise the core," they say. If the
mid-section of the body is not strong,
the body is weakened. It cannot stand
strong, walk tall or balance. The
body is not in alignment with itself.

Without the middle-class, there are
too many heads and too many pairs
of feet wandering helplessly, unable
to stand to full height. All are missing
the mid-section, the power plant that
provides strength and sustenance.

There is no heart.
There is no laughter, joy, and peace
of mind that comes with having
enough: everyone having a fair shot
at making a sustainable living.

Did the computer disembowel the
middle class? Or, was it the incredibly
greedy judgement of human beings?

"The hardest thing about any political campaign is how to win without proving that you are unworthy of winning."

Adlai E. Stevenson

Slap Down

From seventeen plus one, to one.

Walk into any room full of people, deck the first person you see, and watch the others back away.

Most people react fearfully to intimidation and the threat of personal humiliation.

If the bystanders are already filled with anger for the ones being 'slapped down' then they feel vindicated.

The nastier the street fight becomes, the greater the feeling of vindication. The size of the crowds grow in proportion to the vindication they feel: more 'slap downs,' more vindication, greater crowds.

A successful political campaign strategy is born.

The Clown and the Jezebel

The clown car rolled up to the curb.

The clown and the Jezebel got out and introduced themselves as candidates for President of the United States for their respective political parties. Friends before, they would travel on this new path together. Fate, it seemed, had placed them there.

One was a serious candidate, but a lot of people did not believe. They screamed, "No, no, she is a false prophet, a fallen and controlling woman. She cannot be trusted to be in the highest office in the land. She's a Jezebel!"

The other candidate was a clown, but a lot of people did not believe he was a clown, "No, no, he is the real thing. He is truly a God among men, here to deliver us into a life of riches and all things good. Go ahead, ask him, he will tell you so himself."

They travelled down the political path together in the clown car. One with a plan and policies. The other hurling insults at everything our political system represents, "I'll come up with policies when I need them. In the meantime, who else can I disparage?"

Everywhere they travelled, people
cheered: some for, some against,
each candidate.

After their stormy journey
together in the clown car, on
November 8, 2016, they parked
the car and got out.

When the engine cooled,
he was the President-elect.
She was an American Patriot.

Moneyball

Politics by the numbers, the odds:
what plays and where it plays, and
how much does it pay out? If you, or
what you are selling, does not appeal
to one-half of the United States, then
why go there? Why talk to those folks,
if they don't fit in the numbers scheme?

The numbers might project that the
easternmost swath of counties in a
swing state will vote for one candidate
who will go there to reinforce those
voters, try to get them to bring out
more voters, more people like them,
more people like the candidate.

It is known from the numbers
which way these voters lean. The
message will match those leanings
exactly. Why shake any more hands
then is required?

There was a variable that the
algorithms and probabilities
could not measure: the wave.
It was stealthy, under the radar,
i.e., the numbers.

One candidate embraced moneyball,
the other had his hand on the
pulse of the country. One was ruled
by the head. One was ruled by raw
gut instinct.

The numbers, it seems, cannot
measure the intensity and depth
of feeling, desire, disappointment
and disenfranchisement.

In 2016, moneyball did not pay
out according to the numbers.

From Smoke-Filled Rooms to Twitter

Smoke curls up from under the closed
door. A peek inside reveals a handful
of men in a mahogany paneled room:
cigars, laughter, winks, handshakes,
pats on the back for all.

King-makers and policy makers with
motivation, self-interest: an accepted
political practice for many years
producing many kings.

Then, technology snatched the power
from the handful and imparted it to
the 'One.' One man with a Twitter
account and a hand-held instrument
that reached millions in an instant.

The Twitter bait is cast into the waters.
Immediately, fish circle, deciding whether
to take the eye-catching bangle. There
is much flapping and fighting but, in the
end, more fish than not take the bait.

Twitter may be a colorful distraction
to capture or divert our attention. Or,
it could be a method of casting the bait
to have followers perfect the policy
for the leader.

It might be a cutting-edge technique in
the evolution of the Democratic process,
or it could be a masterful technique to
control and subjugate the masses?

Only time will tell.

Just Lie

I wonder if we would ever
teach our children to
'just lie' about anything,
everything. Go ahead and
say whatever you want, dear.

I wonder if I would ever, if I
could ever, give myself permission
to 'just lie' whenever I wanted:
to make a point, to make myself
appear to be more than, greater
than, everyone else.

I wonder how I would feel about
a friend if she/he started to 'just lie'
all the time. Could the love and trust
that was once there endure?
Could I ever just look over the lying?
Let it stand?

Question: How do I feel about a
President who lies all the time?

Answer: My mind cannot expand
widely enough for him to enter.

Fly Overs

At 30,000 feet,
the farm belt looks so pristine:
perfect circles, lush harvest
colors of red, yellow and green.

Everything looks so good down there!

At 30,000 feet,
shuttered factories don't look
shuttered. They look like impressive,
sprawling structures.

Everything looks so good down there!

At 30,000 feet,
the 'Farm for Sale,' 'Foreclosure,' and
'Bank Repossession' signs can't be seen
and neither can the massive numbers
of pink slips issued by the factories.

Everything looks so good down there!

From 30,000 feet,
the plane plummeted, crashed, and
burned. When the smoke cleared, the
cockpit was found in a farmer's circle;
the tail-section crashed through
an abandoned factory.

From 30,000 feet,
everything was not as it appeared to be.

"Logic, sometimes has very little to do with political action."

Alexander Mackenzie

The Russians are Coming!

The United States has influenced elections around the world for generations: toppling a regime here, installing a more favorable leader there. Why would we be surprised that the Russians would be trying to influence our election?

What is surprising, is the collusion with, and pandering to, the Russian government by a presidential candidate. Whose interest is being served and to what end?

Punditry, Press, Fake News

Words matter.
Words can inspire and create, or
words can turn into swords to stab
directly into the heart of Truth.

Punditry or press?

Press denotes professional methods
of investigation: the three-source rule,
for one. Punditry refutes the press:
just open up the mouth and let the
words fly.

The press has morphed
into punditry to win the ratings war:
a disclaimer, "we do not have
confirmation of this, but...."

Every 'news' network spins words
according to their own political
slant.

Enter 'Fake News,' the love child of punditry and 'news.' Anyone can say anything about anything or anyone, and watch it circle the globe in seconds. Any one of us can be a news maker.

Social media holds the keys to this kingdom and the doors are wide open.

The Sacred Trust

Trust, money and power
create a dynamic tension in
government. Trust can get in
the way of the acquisition of
money and power.

Lawmakers set aside trust
in order to accept invitations
from lobbyists to enter into
the cauldron of self-interest.

The sacred trust is a line not to
be crossed without devastating
results. It has been crossed.
Trust is fragile, it does not bend,
it breaks.

Once the line of sacred trust is
breached, faith in the system is
lost. Faith is required to have
sacred trust. When it is no
longer sacred, it is no longer
trust.

Without the sacred trust, there
is no value, no respect. So, then,
why not 'blow it up?'

Drain the Swamp

A promise: to drain the swamp
in Washington, D.C., a murky,
quagmire of politicians, lobbyists,
and operatives of every ilk.

The question is: what is to follow?
Exactly whose swamp is to be drained?
Is it the swamp in my neighbor's backyard?
Or, could it possibly be the swamp in my
own backyard?

The swamp is drained according to a
certain set of beliefs: your swamp is
murky and ugly. But my swamp is so
beautiful, interesting and necessary. My
swamp oxygenates the surroundings, it
spawns new life. It is a critical part of
the eco-system. We would be better off
without your swamp!

Trust is the qualifier for draining the swamp.
If the swamp is drained, will it be replaced
with something better for all, or again for
the limited few?

Or, will the swamp be drained to be
replaced with a black, asphalt parking lot?

The Political Paradigm

The Ship of State pulled out of the harbor on November 9, 2016. It was a brand new shiny ship, sleek and nimble, a yacht really.

It glided smoothly past the homely, rickety barge with government piled high on its deck as cargo. The load balanced precariously on its flat, rusty deck.

The shiny ship captured everyone's attention. It was a sight to behold, while the barge was overloaded, barely afloat. It's crew, skeletal with sunken, disinterested eyes, yelled at the bystanders, "The barge is still the best way to go. It can carry more, we understand it, no need for change. It has churned its way through the water for ages, always arriving at its destination. Who knows what will happen to the new shiny ship when strong winds blow and the seas rage in great turmoil."

The bystanders cheered loudly as they stood and watched the shiny ship disappear into the horizon. Then, they all turned and walked away, without another look at the unsightly, bloated barge.

*"Knowledge of human nature
is the beginning and end
of political education."*

Henry Adams

A New Normal?

As l awakened into consciousness
on November 9, 2016, an unwelcomed
feeling slowly drooled over me: something
of importance would be forever different.
Fear crept up my spine. Was this going to
be my new normal?

No, it would not.

Our political apparatus was in need of an
urgent wake-up call but maybe not one
as drastic and unpredictable as delivered.

If I find it impossible within myself to
believe in the man elected to the highest
office in the land, I will believe, instead, in
the integrity and resilience of our government
as designed and created by our Founding
Fathers to withstand the tests of time.

No matter the ignorance or arrogance
of the man, our government can never
be broken.

From Bubbles to Walls

Already comfortable in my own private bubble, I now need a wall to complete my secluded enclave.

Great care will be given that the wall is beautiful, to complement my bubble. Design and style are so important, maybe the most important aspect of my wall.

The purpose of my bubble is to 'keep in,' while the intent of my wall is to 'keep out.' It is truly a beautiful, symbiotic relationship.

My world is a wonderful place: the temperature is climate controlled, the information received selective, no one else ever wanders past my enclave.

Finally, I am complete: enclosed in my very own bubble; surrounded by my very own wall. I could not have hoped for more.

Me, myself and I.

Bubbles

It appears that we are happier
to be in our own little bubbles
than to be with each other.

When did you last share a cup
of coffee with your neighbor?
Did you know that your neighbor
was one who suffered from a job
layoff, resulting in very different
political opinions from yours?

Could it be that our bubbles
collectively burst on November 8, 2016?
Should we celebrate this newly found
freedom with hot dogs and fireworks?

Warning: Bubbles may not be fit for
human habitation.

Gridlock

Gridlock is a radicalized, ideological black hole. Its purpose is to hold Democracy captive by partisan tactics.

Our Democracy thrives on openness and creative solutions. It was designed to move forward. When the peoples' business is left undone, the pot runs over. It smolders and burns down into the psyche of Americans, leaving charred embers of frustration, anger, resentment.

Those embers ignited in the Presidential election of 2016.

Politicians, take heed. Do your job! You will be gone if you fail to act constructively and productively for the American people. It is not deserved, but you have two more years!

When Did We Become Radicalized?

After violent incidents involving Muslims, the question is always asked, "When did this man become radicalized?"

To radicalize is the process of being pulled into extremes so far that anger and violence is the only answer to any question. We see it so clearly when a Muslim becomes radicalized, loses reason, and is now committed to the death of oneself or other as a means to an end.

Do we, as Americans only look outward: no self-reflection? To look inward doesn't mean that we are weak or feel compelled to apologize for, or to justify our national identity or actions. It means that we are willing to consider methods other than violence.

There are individuals and groups in the United States whose anger is so great as to propel them into violence…NOW.

How did we get so pulled apart, so alienated from each other? How did our beliefs get so radically, opposingly different that we can't even recognize and respect each other as Americans?

When did we become radicalized?

It is Up to Us

It is not the politicians
who will do it.

It is not the press
who will do it.

It is not Wall Street
who will do it.

It is the American people
who will do it.

We will drive the policy.
We will stay vigilant.
We will expect results
from the people elected
to serve us.

That was proven in
the Election of 2016.

The Greater Bargain

Most might agree that Democracy
is a messy business; two steps forward,
one back; circles, and false starts.

The American Democracy, like the lives
it embodies and represents, travels in a
forwardly direction. The intention that
propels us, is the inherent goodness
of the human spirit.

There is a greater bargain, a Covenant,
a commitment to do better, to carry the
best of who we are forward. Americans
will not break this commitment. It is our
sacred destiny to fulfill it.

We will not be afraid. Though we will go
forth with vigilance: to protect, defend
and to advance the best of who we are.

It's More Than Politics

The election is over.
There is a winner and a loser.
For some, to win is not nearly
enough, more is required: smash
her face into the ground, run her
over with a truck; 'Lock Her Up.'
She must be a criminal if she
represents the opposing party.

Politics is more than politics. It is a
big bucket that I put all of my own
stinky trash into. I carry it around
with me, everywhere.

Someone cut me off at the intersection.
Put it in the bucket.

I had to wait in line at the grocery store.
Put it in the bucket.

I lost my cellphone.
Put it in the bucket.

When my bucket is full to running over,
not only will I label it, 'Politics,' I will
have a sub-heading: the candidate's
name of the opposing party. Now, I
can see her face on my bucket.

Then, I will kick and bash the bucket
as if it were the candidate. All of my
personal frustrations will flow out of
me. It feels so good to punch the image
in my mind, of a single person, for whom
I can blame all of my problems.

I can't stop. I am addicted to my own anger.
I can't let go, even though the election is
over....because, it has nothing to do with
politics.

Her Story

She traversed the political
environment for almost half a
century: a citizen advocate and
activist, an elected politician,
and an appointed member of
the President's cabinet.

She went off to college-
A student, while the Vietnam
conflict was raging wildly, she
believed that positive action
could best be accomplished by
working within the system. That
is where she continued to work,
within the system.

She worked for children.
She worked for mothers.
She worked for families.

She went to Arkansas-
She worked to improve education.
She advocated for women in law.
She served on boards.

She went to the White House-
As First Lady, she worked for
universal health care and got
children's health care. She worked
for women's rights as human rights.

She was elected to the Senate-
As senator from New York, she did
not hesitate to cross the aisle and
work with whomever would work
with her. Adoption and foster care
legislation would result.

She was appointed Secretary of State-
She mended fences. There were
lots of fences to mend, world-wide.

She ran for President-
She had always worked within the
system: compromised, parsed, and
bridged conflict. Had she become
the establishment? She was no
longer the wide-eyed, grass-roots
activist. Restless voters were no
longer interested.

The great success, without a doubt,
was the journey, the long road over
which she trod. The intent, the
commitment, the accomplishments
did, in fact, make a difference that
can never be swift boated away.

Hillary's Baggage

An entire eco-system evolved around Hillary's baggage. Its purpose? To insure the healthy growth and continued expansion of the baggage.

If the most investigated person in history, could not get convicted, where's the guilt? If there is no guilt how does the baggage expand exponentially?

Did the observers' perception of reality influence it? So many were so anxious to add to Hillary's baggage, true or not, they didn't care. Pile on more fake news.

The point of the dishonest exercise was to increase the size of the baggage to the point that she would eventually be denied entry because the baggage exceeded the weight limit; the invisible measurement- trust.

Finally, the baggage gained heft, texture, color. It became a valued tangible-trust. People no longer trusted Hillary. The baggage grew from an undefined load to a specific that could be used to undermine her credibility.

Is there a soul alive who doesn't carry baggage?

A Meeting in the Woods

We met
in the woods that day.
Was it by chance? Or did
our feelings pull us that way
to share our pain?

With my daughter on my back,
I voted. I wanted her to be
a part of that historic day:
maybe this time, just maybe.
I and my daughter were so
proud, euphoric and hopeful.

Then,
the wave came and crashed
through our dreams. Others,
too, had hopes and dreams
left unfulfilled.

The wave left us groping for
stability, grabbing at trees,
mud on our faces, bodies
scratched and bruised, psyches
caught in the undertow.

We walked out of it,
my daughter on my back.
Our dreams were in shambles;
our goals in defeat.

We sheltered for a day in the
solace of our home. I cried,
pounded my fists in the air,
fell asleep in total despair.

We awoke to a beautiful day.
Time for a hike in the woods to
cleanse the soul. My daughter,
on my back, was a noticeable
weight today. Autumn leaves
crushed loudly under my feet.

Then,
I saw her as she was cresting the hill
coming toward me; strong feelings
bringing us closer and closer:
defeat, disbelief, bewilderment.

We greeted each other, the pain
in our eyes revealing why we were
there: to share in each other's grief.
We did it in a hug. A picture
of the moment was taken
by a former president.

My daughter is securely on my back,
for now. Perhaps, she will be the
one to lead us out of the woods and,
once again, into our dreams.

April 4th, 1968
MLK

A leader fell, a beloved leader.
A man of immortal stature,
inspirational and courageous;
a life-line to the disenfranchised,
and those who craved equality
and fairness for all.

How could it be?

He led the good fight. He
walked his talk through smoke,
water, and blood. Then, he fell,
by an assassin's bullet.

How to go on?

November 8th, 2016
HRC

I was with her. Now she has been
quieted by an assassin's mouth.
She lives, but left crippled in the
fight with her mirrored opposite.

How could it be?

Those of us with her, a majority
by one count, could not vote our
choice into a position of power.

Not until it happens to you,
do you understand the grief
of losing a leader. The vacuum
left when a shot is fired into
the heart of a movement.

How to go on?

With the life-breath taken away,
we will still survive. It is our nature
to build again, always moving towards....

How Many Votes?

Colorado Caucus chaos, March 1, 2016.
My first vote.

Denver County Convention.
My second vote.

Colorado District Convention.
My third vote.

Colorado State Convention.
My fourth vote.

General election, November 8, 2016.
My fifth vote.

How many votes should it take to elect
the President of the United States?

Doris Ervin
with Barbara Duckworth,
a Colorado Clinton Delegate

"It was my fortune, or misfortune to be called to the office of Chief Executive without any previous political training."

Ulysses S. Grant

www.ingramcontent.com/pod-product-compliance
Lightning Source LLC
Chambersburg PA
CBHW060426050426
42449CB00009B/2157